random heart poetry
first love

mala naidoo

Copyright © 2025 by Mala Naidoo

Publisher: Independent

www.malanaidoo.com

First Published in Australia 2025

The right of Mala Naidoo to be identified as the Author of the Work has been asserted in accordance with the Copyright, Designs and Patents, 1988.

No part of this poetry book may be reproduced in any form or by any electronic or mechanical means, including information storage and retrieval systems, without written permission from the author, except for the use of brief quotations in a book review.

Naidoo, Mala

Title: *Random Heart Poetry: First Love*

Print ISBN: 978-0-6455450-7-4

A Mother's Love Liberates

— Maya Angelo

about the author

Mala Naidoo is an Australian author. She has worked as an educator in Australia, and South Africa during the grip of apartheid atrocities, and the early days of its dismantling. Mala Naidoo upholds *justice for all* in her novels, short stories and poems on culture, race, gender, and identity. Her writing mission is: *in our angst and joy we are ONE under the Sky of Humanity*

*In memory of my beloved mother who lived a selfless faith-filled life,
cherishing and serving family and community.
~MN*

first love
. . .

we heard your soft melody
so sweetly sung to us
snug and secure in utero
swaying to your rhythm
as you waited and anticipated
then your unknown
cherished babes
born from love into love
from darkness to light
from you to now
mother our songbird
forevermore

haiku 1
. . .

her selfless love gives
breath to her beloved child
mother you are life

galaxy of love
. . .

our home of yesteryear
a magnet to many in angst or joy
mother of many
embraced as your own
golden showers wrapped
in a galaxy of love divine
drawn from the heart and soul
of the Supreme Mother
advice you shared
a warm plate you offered
to touch and heal
like only a mother can

your needs never spoken
smiling lips—the language
of your inner being

none to compare

nurse
. . .

a little frame and curious mind
reading well into the night
devouring books at the speed of light

swift and deft of foot is she
moving with the graceful ease of flight
multi-tasking and forever bright

a selfless nurse in her day
voluntarily serving many forsaken
by a system prohibiting equality

bringing wellness
to body, mind and soul
filling incapacitation's begging bowl

divine mother
. . .

a woman of strength, dignity and grace
moonlight radiates through her
tender lion heart
resilience born from life's rocky road

she is the river and the ocean
the fountain of life's ebb and flow
leading the way in rhythmic sway
sunbeams sparkle across streams
nodding to cosmic beauty rich and rare

she is the music in every child's song
her sweet melody the lullaby
soothing tears
stitching a broken soul
mending a tattered smile

she is the dance—a waltz through time

Athena, Kali, Parvati, Ungamilia, Yemaya
she is Mother and we are Her
The Mother Divine

haiku 2

. . .

up the summer hill
she trudged laden with parcels
after day's frail care

mother and child
. . .

when I looked into your eyes
for the very first time
our eyes locked
mine on your comforting beauty
that over-swelled my heart's space
newborn skin
and unfurling fingers and toes
downy black hair
smooth on her babes delicate heads

as days passed
her heart lurched

first smile
first tooth
first word
first step
first heartbreak

now we laugh late into the night
her smile wide her eyes bright
her first joy—her first love—now endless
a mother's ceaseless love

grief
. . .

three months—gone—since you departed
your physical absence a palpable void

but memories of you live on my darling
surrounded by the gentle glow of you
bathed in warm smiles
the comfort of your humble aura prevails
in selfless lived and shared wisdom

the stories told of a time long gone
when all the world lived as one...

mama africa

. . .

dewy mornings, hot days, warm nights
lush rolling hills and starry skies
graceful impala, giraffe and springbok
adorn the african savannah

down in the valley
smoke trickles atop thatched roofs
eyes blink open to sun's first rays
pap froths over radiant golden coals
lighting up and warming
a day ready to be received

her rainbow streaked scarf
twirled to crown her regal head
flowing down the back of her swishing gown
awash with nature's brushstrokes
teases her ankles

she hums the song of motherhood
soothing and protecting
loving and supporting
nourishing and growing

her babies adorn her beloved landscape

admiration

. . .

i admired you in silence
awed by your strength
beauty and wisdom
wanting and fearing
introversion my forever Achilles' Heel
sensing and knowing my spirit
you showered tough love
coaxing me to raise my fearful head
buried between my feet
to feel the sun upon my face
to unfurl closed petals within
to let my voice ascend
across mountaintops

'justice' you said, 'must be sought'
'be bold, reach for the stars'
'speak your truth but once'

today, i continue to sing
your praises
forever in awe
seeking the cloudless sky in you

goodwill ancestry

. . .

grandfather
in every way a goodwill gentleman
tailor-fitted in the finest fabric
polished manner to match

an astute restauranteur
and a loving family man
serving the Durban non-white hub
world class cuisine in regal style

a grand man—a community icon
a meld of east and west
he left an indelible memory
that race nor creed could mar

goodwill lounge—his trademark
many a black artist launched
to find a soulful musical home
beyond the bars of law

grandfather left his mark
on beloved mama
shaping class and style
humility and joy in serving all

goodwill was your genetic hallmark
in how you moved with ease and grace
among those who needed you most

grandmother
bore an inner and physical strength
undefined by era
stoic in every way
faith, culture and tradition upheld
seamlessly stitched
into the depths of your soul

nothing but the best she expected
giving her all to protect her offspring
to hold their own in life's hemispheres

haiku 3
. . .

a magical touch
flourishing divine green thumb
grows a paradise

childhood home
. . .

an open home to many
a haven to bleeding souls
bent and broken
by societal pressure
your comfort assured knew no bounds
advice offered drawn from truth
those who walked in dusty shadows
kindly led to self-assess, cleanse and mend
finding a permanent place
in her adopted parental embrace

but those hurt by human cruelty
assured unyielding maternal affection
entering a doorway open for their return
greeted by the touch of a welcome smile

a seat set at the supper table
invited to break bread from the family plate
childhood home to all and many
many and more

sunday mornings
. . .

freshly baked bread wafts
prodding olfactory senses
in semi-conscious inhalation
rising yeast and toasting sesame seeds
a languishing child's nirvana

a tiptoe to the oven door
a sight for half-sleepy eyes to behold!
bread rolls puffed with pride
tease in golden delight
for a drooling gustatory bite

at the breakfast table set for four
morning tea awaits
as oozing butter seeps into fluffy clouds
of piping hot crusty bread

then the rush to dress in sunday's best
toppling into the family car
the silent ride to sunday school

mother chants a mantra—setting the mood
for a morning filled with sweet melodies
and divine tales to uplift the soul

the week is made
ignited by faith
brightened with the light of maternal love

meditative mood
. . .

early morn solitude—meandering mind
seeking inner space
searching...yearning confirmation

a distant harp strain carries
the ocean's salt-drenched breeze
as a motherly touch across the face
a faint floral hint inhaled

silence in floating sensations
stealthy shutters of the inner eye rise
light teases—lingers and widens
a vivid vision—one slide at a time

your rapturous smile
your luminescent eyes
the inner being moves to face the light
encircling your ethereal presence
beads pass through fervent fingers
lips mouth the chant
in clockless time

peace permeates in unimaginable calm

you are well and safe—breathing the air of heaven

that is all I need know
until we meet again

life's circle
. . .

in frail aging years
constant companions we were
laughing or sharing solitude
in meditative hours

then reminiscing about life past
the country folk of yesteryear
heartwarming neighbours
sharing celebratory cultural connections
since time immemorial
childhood camping trips
the oneness of friends bound together
united in faith-filled purpose

now I see you in butterfly prances
feel you in the breeze of early morn
at the first peep of sunlight
at days end nestled among the stars

a whisper beckons every so often
charting life's course, guiding actions
while tending heaven's garden

starlit
. . .

twinkling stars wink in the heavens
the universe alight under a night sky
soothing the aching, lingering yearning

arms reaching down
in a mother's embrace
girdling a fractured soul
in an unfathomable presence

all seeing all knowing

aloft a starlit velvet expanse
scintillating stars collectively sparkle
revealing the radiance of your visage
gleaming from moonlit eyes

gratitude
. . .

thank you for leading the way
putting others first
for kindness and compassion

nurse, mother, wife, grandmother, sister
aunt, daughter-in-law, sister-in-law
mother-in-law and best friend

a listening ear for all who needed you
your tender warm touch lives on

a seat left empty in our family home
but oceans of heartwarming memories
arise each hour
to caress our aching hearts
warm our days and nights

gone but never forgotten

ringing bells
. . .

bells ring out
announcing the passing of a great soul
cherished in this earthbound sojourn

the full circumference ends
three hundred and sixty degrees
complete circle of life attained

a heavenly hearth
awaits the allotted hour
the endpoint of the final journey
no human hand can halt

the mystery of life
the cycle of birth and death
the ultimate transition
through time and space

fear not the ringing bells
time's wingèd chariot awaits
the return to the ultimate abode
at the feet of the divine

elfchen

. . .

mother
sweet mother
her children first
led by divine love
cherished

The Mother of the Universe is the Mother of All
　—Holy Mother

afterword

Poetry says much in a few short lines. It is a literary form that enhances all other writing if observed for the depth and clarity it brings. From reading and teaching poetry emerged the inspiration to handwrite poems as they arrived in the conscious mind. Now it's the glue that holds my writing life together.

If you are an aspiring poet here is my take on why poetry matters in composing prose.

Poetry Educates Prose

Poet or novelist, one, the other or both—one grows into the other almost instinctively to develop the ideal creative state.

Writing improves with consistency and ongoing learning of the essentials of the craft. The art of writing expands the imagination and bulks the creative muscle by triggering the desire to know more, to research, to read, to push boundaries, and feel joy —the perpetual quest of the writer.

Voracious reading of all forms and more particularly poetry, the fine art of saying much succinctly, is a skill worth learning to enhance prose writing skills. Poetry as a literary form is laden with layered sensory imagery, conveying pain and joy, the state of the human condition and a celebration of nature which when emulated in prose fiction, is the *lyricism in narration* or the *cadence of poetic storytelling*.

The habit of reading poetry grows the writer's ability to choose appropriate/effective language or specific words that says it all with brevity and simplicity. We live in an era where attention span is brief, access is quick, and impatience governs desires.

Little bursts remain to sustain...

There is an intensely intimate, mindful experience apparent in poetry, a purity that makes it more personal where prose is more social, and when married with a sensitivity to both forms, the reader benefits from the writer's authenticity.

As a teacher, evidence suggests that incremental learning leads to lifelong knowledge. Piecemeal understanding is committed to memory in meaningful short bursts as opposed to lengthy mindless memorisation that disappears after the moment of recall.

Poetry speaks in the rhythm and profundity of its brief lines, a boon in holding the attention of the reader.

Poetry read before sitting down to write prose, or read as the last activity before sleep sharpens the ability to borrow from the poetic form and style for precise, well-formed ideas that touch with the depth and clarity that poetry engenders.

If writing in a particular genre or establishing an emotion in a prose scene, turn to poetry that's appropriate in that instant and feel the passion and power of the words and those left unsaid, then a deepening of thought processes emerge to heighten the imagination. Reading poetry written in any period has the inspirational ability to enhance overall writing.

Crafting poems for creative leisure or publication is beneficial as self-directed editing of what works and what requires reworking. Poetry cannot hide intention and purpose, it's stark, it's true, a visual and emotive painting through words. This skill shapes brilliance in prose writing.

Poetry and prose are close cousins of the writing family. Read as many novels as you would poems, or more to capture that sweet spot of simple, short, stunning sentences, one after the other, until a story is born.

How many poetry books are there on your bookshelf? The internet is a valuable source, but there's much to be said on having a book in your hand as you read, delight in, make note of, absorb and contemplate.

For aspiring writers: Write a poem today on any topic, let it tumble freely onto the page, then try your hand at prose. Watch the magic unfold. An open mind is necessary to attain this joy, and brilliance in prose writing.

If you have enjoyed reading my poems please leave a review on your chosen platform so that other readers might find my random heart and linger among and between the words in this collection… for a while.

With gratitude,

Mala
www.malanaidoo.com

also by mala naidoo

Novels:

Across Time and Space

Vindication Across Time

Souls of Her Daughters

Chosen Lives

What Change May Come

Aurora Days

Gallery Nights

Blackwater Mornings

Plantation Shadows

Short Stories:

The Rain

Life's Seasons

Crossings

Poetry:

Random Heart Poetry : Light and Shade

Random Heart Poetry : Visions and Voices

Random Heart Poetry : Time and Place

Random Heart Poetry : Rainbows and Shards

www.ingramcontent.com/pod-product-compliance
Lightning Source LLC
Chambersburg PA
CBHW022022290426
44109CB00015B/1282